USING A
SCALE

By Nora Roman

Please visit our website, www.garethstevens.com. For a free color catalog of all our high-quality books, call toll free 1-800-542-2595 or fax 1-877-542-2596.

Library of Congress Cataloging-in-Publication Data

Names: Roman, Nora (Children's author), author.
Title: Using a scale / Nora Roman.
Description: New York : Gareth Stevens Publishing, [2018] | Series: Super science tools | Includes bibliographical references and index.
Identifiers: LCCN 2016056097| ISBN 9781482464054 (pbk. book) | ISBN 9781482464061 (6 pack) | ISBN 9781482464078 (library bound book)
Subjects: LCSH: Scales (Weighing instruments)–Juvenile literature. | Measurement–Juvenile literature.
Classification: LCC QC107 .R66 2018 | DDC 681.2–dc23
LC record available at https://lccn.loc.gov/2016056097

Published in 2018 by
Gareth Stevens Publishing
111 East 14th Street, Suite 349
New York, NY 10003

Copyright © 2018 Gareth Stevens Publishing

Designer: Laura Bowen
Editor: Therese Shea

Photo credits: Cover, p. 1 fstop123/Getty Images; pp. 1–24 (series art) T.Sumaetho/ Shutterstock.com; p. 5 (top) kali9/Getty Images; p. 5 (bottom) Seregraff/Shutterstock.com; p. 7 MNStudio/Shutterstock.com; p. 9 Steve Pepple/Shutterstock.com; p. 11 Digital Light Source/ Universal Images Group/Getty Images; p. 13 Ivonne Wierink/Shutterstock.com; p. 15 Westend61/ Getty Images; p. 17 Jonathan Pow/Getty Images; p. 19 phloxii/Shutterstock.com; p. 21 (scale) Maglara/Shutterstock.com; p. 21 (boy) Jack Frog/Shutterstock.com.

Printed in the United States of America

CPSIA compliance information: Batch #CS17GS: For further information contact Gareth Stevens, New York, New York at 1-800-542-2595.

CONTENTS

Boldface words appear in the glossary.

A Way to Weigh

Picture yourself at a carnival. There's a fun ride you want to try. However, the rules say you must weigh at least 50 pounds (23 kg) to ride. You're not sure you do. How can you find out? Use a scale!

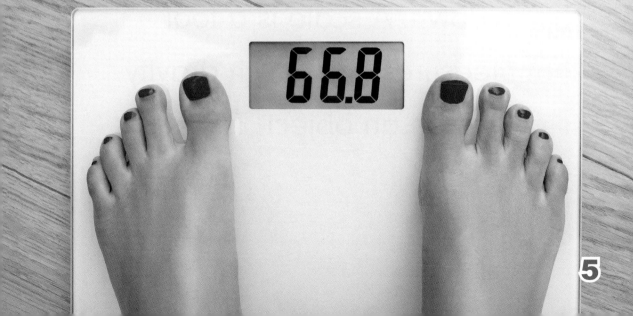

5

Great Gravity!

Everything on Earth with **mass** has weight because of gravity. Gravity is the force that pulls things down. A scale is a tool that measures how much gravity is pulling on an object. That's its weight!

Spring Scales

You might have a spring scale in your bathroom. When you step onto it, you press down a spring beneath the top of the scale. That moves a pointer to a number. The number is your weight!

Balance Scales

A **balance** scale has a beam, or bar, with a tray hanging from or resting on each side. You can place objects in each tray to find out which weighs more. When the trays are balanced, the objects weigh the same.

The balance scale on the next page shows how to use an object called a known weight. Some known weights have their weight written on them! Place the weight or weights on one tray. Then add objects to the other tray until the trays balance. Now you know the weight of both trays.

13

In the Lab

Scientists have to be exact. Adding too much or too little of something can make a difference in their **experiments**. Even the smallest bit can change results. Scientists often use a scale called a top-loading balance.

15

Some scales are **digital** so measurements are more exact. In the United States, weight is sometimes measured using **units** such as ounces and pounds. Other countries use **metric** units such as grams and kilograms. Scientists do, too.

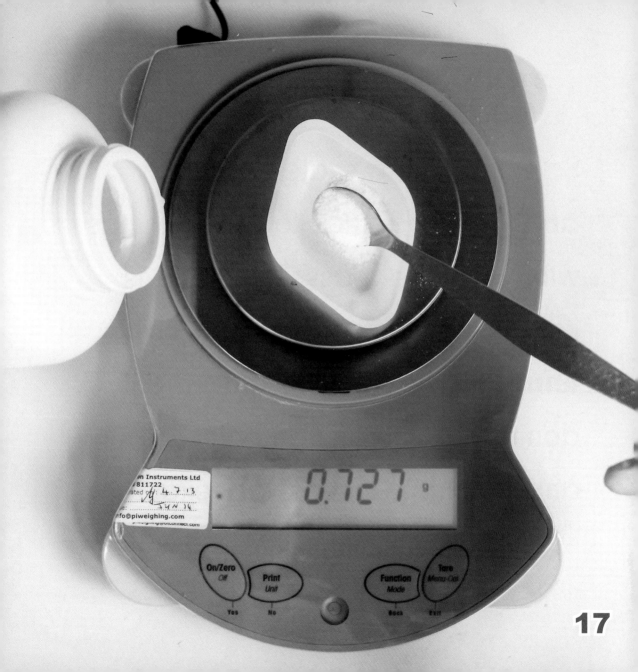

On/Zero
Off

Print
Unit

Function
Mode

Tare
Menu-Cal

Yes

No

Back

Exit

n Instruments Ltd
811722
rated off: 4.7.13.
2: .... JUN 14.
nfo@piweighing.com
.com

0.727 g

17

Scientists use a scale called an **analytical** balance to weigh things with very little mass. The scale is kept in a glass case so that dust, **temperature**, and air movement don't affect measurements. The analytical balance is very exact.

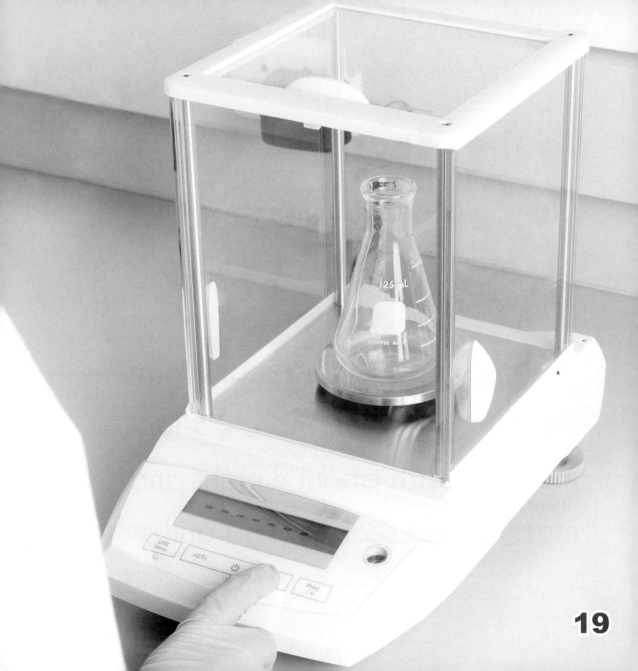

19

To the Moon!

Did you know that you'd weigh less on the moon than you do on Earth? That's because the moon has less gravity! Your mass remains the same, though. There's a lot more to learn about weight and mass. Use a scale to find out!

You Use Scales!

1) Use a kitchen or bathroom scale to weigh five things at home.

2) Write them in order, from lightest to heaviest.

21

GLOSSARY

analytical: having to do with the careful study of something

balance: having to do with having equal amounts of something

digital: showing numbers rather than using hands or a pointer

experiment: a scientific test in which you perform actions and carefully watch their results in order to learn about something

mass: the amount of matter in something

metric: having to do with the system of weights and measures that is based on the meter and gram

temperature: how hot or cold something is

unit: an amount of length, weight, time, or money that is used as a standard for counting or measuring

FOR MORE INFORMATION

BOOKS

Gardner, Robert. *How Heavy Is Heavy? Science Projects with Weight.* Berkeley Heights, NJ: Enslow Elementary, 2015.

Metz, Lorijo. *Using Scales and Balances.* New York, NY: PowerKids Press, 2013.

Pipe, Jim. *Balancing: Cranes, Scales, and Seesaws.* North Mankato, MN: Stargazer Books, 2008.

WEBSITES

Gravity: Facts
idahoptv.org/sciencetrek/topics/gravity/facts.cfm
Find out more about gravity, mass, and weight here.

Measuring Matter
brainpop.com/science/matterandchemistry/measuringmatter/
Read different ways to measure matter.

INDEX